SEAHORSES

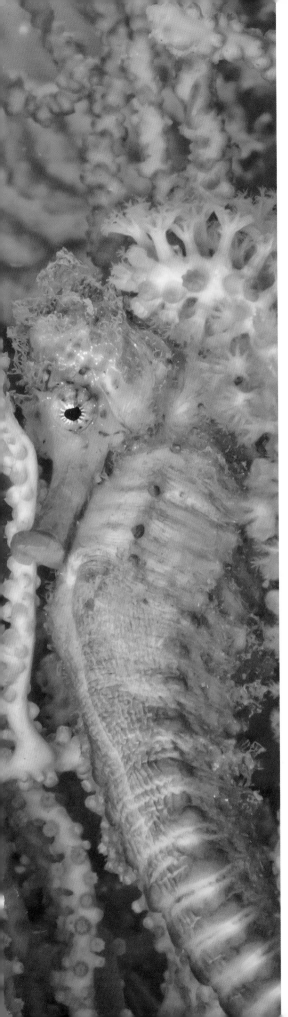

LIVING WILD

Published by Creative Education and Creative Paperbacks
P.O. Box 227, Mankato, Minnesota 56002
Creative Education and Creative Paperbacks are imprints of The Creative Company
www.thecreativecompany.us

Design and production by Mary Herrmann
Art direction by Rita Marshall
Printed in China

Photographs by Alamy (Images & Stories), Creative Commons Wikimedia (Frederick Stuart Church, Jennifer Dunne/Flickr, Bernard DUPONT/Flickr, Brian Gratwicke/Flickr, Aaron Gustafson/Flickr, Hans Hillewaert, Nick Hobgood, JMiall/British Museum, Los Angeles County Museum of Art, Mark Norman/Museum Victoria, Operational Land Imager/NASA, Reto Pieren, prilfish/Flickr, H. Zell), Dreamstime (Creativefire, Eugenesergeev, jordieasy, Kelpfish, PureSolution, Wrangel, Zepherwind), Getty Images (HNH Images), iStockphoto (Divography, Steve Lovegrove, MadKruben), Shutterstock (Rostislav Ageev, Andaman, Anna Andych, atiger, Dray van Beeck, Kjeld Friis, Frolova_Elena, Abd. Halim Hadi, Matej Kastelic, Visun Khankasem, littlesam, CK Ma, MaeManee, Gerald Marella, Antonio Martin, Veronika Matejkova, miminoshka, Christian Mueller, NA image, Nine_Tomorrows, omers, phugunfire, Pille, Ekkapan Poddamrong, scubaluna, Kristina Vackova)

Library of Congress Cataloging-in-Publication Data
Names: Gish, Melissa, author.
Title: Seahorses / Melissa Gish.
Series: Living wild.
Includes bibliographical references and index.
Summary: A look at seahorses, including their habitats, physical characteristics such as their prehensile tails, behaviors, relationships with humans, and the mysteries that still surround these fish today.
Identifiers: LCCN 2016036686 / ISBN 978-1-60818-834-5 (hardcover) / ISBN 978-1-62832-437-2 (pbk) / ISBN 978-1-56660-882-4 (eBook)
Subjects: LCSH: Seahorses—Juvenile literature.
Classification: LCC QL638.S9 G57 2017 / DDC 597/.6798—dc23

CCSS: RI.5.1, 2, 3, 8; RST.6-8.1, 2, 5, 6, 8; RH.6-8.3, 4, 5, 6, 7, 8

First Edition HC 9 8 7 6 5 4 3 2 1
First Edition PBK 9 8 7 6 5 4 3 2 1

CREATIVE EDUCATION • CREATIVE PAPERBACKS

SEAHORSES

Melissa Gish

The morning sun penetrates the sea,
illuminating Osprey Reef like a flowering

underwater garden. Hidden among the lacy sea fans are dozens of tiny seahorses.

The morning sun penetrates the sea, illuminating Osprey Reef like a flowering underwater garden. Hidden among the lacy sea fans are dozens of tiny seahorses. Mimicking the color and knobby appearance of the structures to which they cling, these Denise's pygmy seahorses are barely visible. The waters surrounding the reef, located northeast of Queensland, Australia, are warm, calm, and crystal clear. Whitetip reef sharks leisurely cruise among the corals and gorgonian sea fans. Triggerfish hunt crabs in the shadows, while a dogtooth tuna stalks a school of yellowback fusiliers. None of these predators is aware of the pygmy seahorses clutching to the pink sea fans. Their tails providing a firm grip, these colorful seahorses blend perfectly into their habitat. They sway gently to and fro, ingesting minuscule **zooplankton** that drift within reach. The seahorses will live their entire lives on the sea fans, going mostly unnoticed by their neighbors on the reef.

WHERE IN THE WORLD THEY LIVE

■ **Pot-bellied Seahorse**
Australia and New Zealand

■ **Barbour's Seahorse**
Indonesia, Malaysia, Philippines

■ **Bargibant's Pygmy Seahorse**
from Japan to Australia

■ **Jayakar's Seahorse**
Indian Ocean near Oman, Israel, and Pakistan

■ **Pacific Seahorse**
from California to northern South America

Because of their small size and ability to blend in with surroundings, the more than 50 species of seahorse are often difficult to find in the world's oceans. New species continue to be discovered. The colored squares represent known locations of selected species living in the wild today.

■ **Lined Seahorse**
Atlantic Ocean from Canada to Venezuela

■ **Cape Seahorse**
southern coast of South Africa

■ **Spiny Seahorse**
central and western Pacific; Indian Ocean

STRANGE SWIMMING HORSES

Leafy seadragons live in coastal waters of southern and western Australia, where they are nicknamed "leafies."

Seahorses have a reputation for magic and mystery that makes them familiar all around the world. With armored bodies, monkey-like tails, horselike heads, and trumpet-shaped snouts, these fish seem otherworldly. They belong to the family Syngnathidae, which also includes pipefish and seadragons. The family name is derived from the Greek *syn*, meaning "fused" and *gnathus*, meaning "jaw." All fish in this family have jaws that do not open. Seahorses belong to the genus *Hippocampus*. Also Greek, *hippo* means "horse," and *kampos* means "sea monster." Seahorses are certainly strange, but they are far from monstrous. The largest seahorse ever recorded was barely more than 13 inches (33 cm) long.

More than 50 seahorse species have been named, and new species are still being discovered. Seahorses vary greatly in size, shape, and color. At less than one inch (2.5 cm) long, the seven species of pygmy seahorses are the smallest. The Satomi's pygmy seahorse, discovered in 2008, is the smallest—the size of one M&M's® candy. The largest seahorse species, the pot-bellied seahorse, is nearly 30 times bigger, averaging 12 inches (30.5 cm) in length.

Hippocampus waleananus, unofficially known as the Walea soft coral seahorse, has the longest tail of any pygmy seahorse.

Each seahorse's coronet is unique— like human fingerprints, coronets can be used to identify individual seahorses.

Seahorses live in most of the world's oceans and inhabit a variety of environments, from the open sea to shallow coastal waters and **estuaries**. Some species are endemic to their habitats, meaning they are found nowhere else on Earth. The knobby, bullneck, narrow-bellied, and zebra seahorses are endemic to Australia. The Shiho's and crowned seahorses are found only in Japan, while the Cape seahorse is endemic to the southern coast of South Africa.

Other species have vast ranges. The spiny seahorse is found from southern Russia to Australia to the eastern coast of Africa. The Pacific seahorse ranges from San Diego, California, to Peru and the Galápagos Islands. And the lined seahorse can be found in the Atlantic Ocean from Canada to the Bahamas to Brazil. Some species are so rare that they are known only from a single individual and have no common name. *Hippocampus tyro* was found off the coast of the East African island of Seychelles, and *Hippocampus waleananus* was discovered in 2009 in the Togian Islands, near Indonesia.

Unlike most other fish, seahorses do not have scales. Instead, their skin is stretched over bony rings throughout

The seahorse's fins may appear fragile, but they are incredibly strong, beating thousands of times every minute.

Even when contending with powerful and fast currents, the seahorse can anchor itself with its muscular tail.

their bodies. Each species has a specific number of rings. Seahorse bodies consist of three main sections: the head, trunk, and tail. Like most bony fishes, seahorses have a swim bladder, which is a gas-filled sac that regulates the fish's **buoyancy** and keeps it afloat when it isn't moving. Because seahorses eat almost nonstop, the cycle of digestion and absorption of **nutrients** runs continuously. A long intestine begins in the snout and runs the length of the trunk. The seahorse has no stomach. Its tiny heart pumps blood through the body, and a liver, a urine bladder, and kidneys filter waste.

Seahorses have two eyes—one on each side of the head. This gives them full 360-degree vision. The eyes can be rotated independently of each other, allowing the seahorse to look in two different directions at once. To see clearly, however, the seahorse must focus with both eyes. Some seahorse species can see objects from as far away as 15 feet (4.6 m). The snout length varies depending on species. Seahorses have no teeth. They use their snout like a straw to suck up tiny animals that swim or float nearby. The top of the seahorse's head is called the coronet, which is derived from a French word meaning

Having eyes that can look in two different directions at the same time doubles the seahorse's chance of finding food.

Tiger tail seahorses live in waters around Malaysia, Singapore, Thailand, Vietnam, and the Philippines.

Small seahorses have a shorter life span than large ones: dwarf seahorses live about one year, but pot-bellied seahorses can live five years.

"crown." The coronet can be low and fairly smooth, or it can be tall with prominent points.

Like all fish, seahorses breathe through slits called gills. Pygmy seahorses have one gill on the back of the head, but other seahorses have a pair of gills that look like puffy cheeks. Water flows through the gills, where thin **membranes** collect oxygen and transfer it to the seahorse's bloodstream. Just behind the gills are the pectoral fins. The fluttering motion of these fan-shaped limbs propels the seahorse through the water. The tiny anal fin, located just above the tail on the front of the trunk, and the long dorsal fin on the back of the trunk help the seahorse maneuver. The pectoral fins can flutter up to 50 times per second, and the dorsal fin can flutter up to 35 times per second. Seahorses swim upright, which makes them very slow. The *Guinness Book of World Records* lists the world's slowest fish as the dwarf seahorse, which can swim only five feet (1.5 m) per hour.

A seahorse's body may be covered with only the bony ridges from its rings, or it could have additional bumps, called tubercles. These may be additional points of bone attached to the seahorse's rings, or they may be fleshy

Coleman's pygmy seahorse, found only around Lord Howe Island, Australia, is just 0.9 inch (2.3 cm) long.

Visitors are allowed to touch and interact with seahorses at the Ocean Rider Seahorse Farm in Kailua-Kona, Hawaii.

bumps growing on the skin. Spindly appendages, called cirri, may exist among the bony ridges and tubercles. The appearance of cirri varies by species as well as environment. If seahorses need a lot of **camouflage**, they may grow a lot of cirri. Captive seahorses, experiencing no danger from predators, tend to have few cirri. Seahorses can grow and shed cirri at will. The Brazilian seahorse has no cirri, while the Barbour's seahorse of Indonesia, Malaysia, and the Philippines has long, elaborate cirri.

The seahorse's body is covered with slime that protects the fish from disease and helps it retain water inside its body. This slime, produced by **glands** beneath the skin, also encourages the growth of algae on the skin. Since they are not strong swimmers, seahorses rely on the algae to attract zooplankton prey and to provide additional camouflage from predators. The seahorse has a long, **prehensile** tail that curls around corals like a hand. Its tail is not round like other animals'. Rather, it has square corners. In creating robot models of various animal tails, scientists at the University of Oregon discovered that the seahorse's square-shaped tail is much stronger than round tails, making it far less likely to break when pulled.

The softcoral seahorse, discovered in the Red Sea off the coast of Egypt in 2009, is about as long as a paper clip.

Lined seahorses normally inhabit shallow, grassy bays in summer and then retreat to deeper water in winter.

A POCKET FULL OF FRY

Some seahorse species are territorial and prefer to live alone, while others are social and find safety in numbers.

Found from the Philippines to Australia, the winged seahorse is named for the pair of winglike spines found along its back.

Most seahorses live their entire lives in a single small territory. Large seahorses may roam an area of seagrass the size of a bathtub, while small seahorses barely move from a single finger-sized branch of sea fan. Regardless of size, seahorses defend their territory from intruders. When they fight, seahorses typically entangle their tails and try to pull each other away from the territory. They may also butt heads like minuscule bighorn sheep until one of them gives up and swims away. Males are especially territorial during mating season.

When the time comes to reproduce, a female seahorse roams from one male's territory to another's looking for a mate. When she finds a male without a mate, she lets him know that she is available by swimming within his territory. If he accepts her, they will become a pair for the entire mating season. This season can last up to eight months, usually from mid-February to late October. If one member of the pair is killed, the other may have to wait for the next mating season to find a new mate. Some dwarf and pygmy species mate year-round, so, in essence, these two groups of seahorses mate for life.

Unlike most seahorses, pot-bellied seahorses are strong swimmers and may travel several hundred yards in one day.

While newborn pygmy seahorses are microscopic, newborn pot-bellied seahorses are larger than adult pygmy seahorses!

Males have longer bodies and tails than females. Males also have something females lack: a brood pouch. This structure on the outside of the body makes seahorses, pipefish, and seadragons unique in the animal world. The male—not the female—becomes pregnant with offspring. Similar to female kangaroos, male seahorses have a pouch where their young develop. One exception is the group of pygmy seahorses. These seahorses are so small that they do not have a pouch. Instead, male pygmy seahorses incubate their eggs inside the body.

Mating begins with an elaborate morning courtship ritual that strengthens the pair's bond. The seahorses begin by wrapping their tails around the same anchor. Then they change color, becoming bright, and take turns vibrating their bodies. Next, they release their grip just enough to swing in circles around their anchor. The seahorses do this for one to three mornings in a row to establish their relationship and prepare their bodies for mating. Once they are ready to mate, the female faces the male and points her head upward. In response, the male vibrates his body and points his head upward. Then the pair swims upward and downward several times, facing

each other. When they are properly positioned, they entwine their tails. The female then transfers her eggs into the male's brood pouch.

After mating, the male rocks back and forth, settling the eggs inside his pouch. The eggs stick to the inside walls of the pouch, where a protective, spongy tissue grows around them. Each egg has a yolk, which nourishes the baby seahorse, called a fry. The male's body also provides **hormones** and additional nutrients to help the fry develop. Depending on the species, a seahorse may hold from 5 to 2,500 eggs in its pouch.

The length of time it takes for the eggs to develop,

Seahorses' courtship and mating process involves a long and complex series of bonding behaviors.

Groups of seahorses traveling together are commonly called herds, while groups that stay in one place are called colonies.

called the gestation period, varies by species. Dwarf and pygmy seahorses develop in about 10 days. Lined seahorses take about 15 days, and pot-bellied seahorses require 25 days to develop. The female remains a faithful companion throughout the gestation period, visiting her partner every morning. They entwine tails around an anchor and swim together in circles for a while before the female goes off to feed. While the male is incubating the eggs, the female is preparing the next batch of eggs in her own body. In this way, the male seahorse can become pregnant again within hours or days of giving birth.

When the time comes for the fry to be born, the male's pouch opens and the fry are spewed out. They are fully formed, tiny versions of their parents. Most are swept away and become food for larger animals, but many find an anchor and begin feeding immediately. They will reach adulthood at 2 to 12 months, depending on the species. Only about 0.5 percent of all seahorse fry survive long enough to mate and continue the cycle of life.

Unlike many other fish, seahorses do not swim in schools. Living alone or in pairs, they are especially vulnerable to predators such as seabirds, sea turtles, crabs,

Pygmy seahorse bodies have tubercles and colors that mimic the coral on which they live, rendering them nearly invisible.

Because seahorses will not eat dead prey, captive seahorses are typically fed live mysids (pictured), krill, or brine shrimp.

rays, skates, sharks, tuna, and other carnivorous fish. Seahorses rely on camouflage for protection from these predators. To better hide among plants, corals, and rocks, seahorses not only grow cirri but also change color. Their skin is covered with chromatophores, which are tiny cells containing yellow, red, orange, and black **pigments**. Each chromatophore is controlled by a nerve and a muscle. The seahorse's brain sends a signal along the nerve to tell the muscle to contract. This muscle contraction causes the chromatophore to change color.

Seahorses change color for a variety of reasons aside from camouflage. They become bright colors when excited or curious, and dark when stressed or exposed to light that is brighter than normal. Seahorses' colors can also indicate the quality of their environment. Their colors fade—even to white—if the water temperature is higher than normal, the oxygen level is too low, or the water contains **contaminants**. Researchers have learned that seahorses are highly sensitive to changes in water quality. Pollution from human activities and the effects of global **climate change** on the world's oceans are negatively affecting seahorse health.

To survive, seahorses require a healthy **ecosystem** that produces abundant zooplankton, including mysids, also called opossum shrimp. Of the more than 1,000 mysid species, none is more than 1 inch (2.5 cm) long, and many are microscopic. Some seahorses can eat as many as 3,000 organisms per day. Most seahorse species are active only during daylight. At night, they anchor themselves securely with their tails and go to sleep, sometimes even lying down on their anchors. Seahorses do not have eyelids, so their eyes are always open, even when they are sleeping. Bright light disturbs their sleep, so captive seahorses under artificial light must be allowed to experience daytime and nighttime.

It may be difficult to determine when a seahorse is sleeping, but its relaxed posture is one clue.

CLEMENS XII · PONT · MAX ·
AQVAM VIRGINEM
COPIA ET SALVBRITATE COMMENDATAM
CVLTV MAGNIFICO ORNAVIT
ANNO DOMINI MDCCXXXV · PONTIF · VI ·

PERFECIT · BENEDICTVS XIV · PON · MAX ·

In 1998, the Trevi Fountain was cleaned, its cracks were skillfully repaired, and its marble surfaces were polished.

MAGIC AND MYSTERY

The sea is a vast, mysterious place inhabited by wondrous creatures, such as seahorses, that have inspired legends the world over. One of the most famous sea creatures comes from ancient Greek **mythology**. The hippocamp is a mythical beast with the head, neck, and front legs of a horse and the lower body of a seahorse. Poseidon, the Greek god of the ocean, commanded the hippocamps. He rode them, and they pulled his chariot. His favorite hippocamps were named Skylla and Sthenios. Poseidon's son, Triton, and magical sea nymphs—fairy-like beings called Nereids—also rode hippocamps.

When the Romans conquered Greece in the second century B.C., they adopted many Greek traditions. Poseidon became known as Neptune in Roman mythology. Epic poems were written about Neptune and the hippocamp that he rode. Hippocamps were depicted in elaborate tile **mosaics**, and their images were painted on pottery and stamped on coins. Gold and silver were shaped into hippocamp jewelry, and marble was carved into hippocamp statues. Some hippocamps are depicted with wings, including those that are part of *Trevi Fountain* in

Stories of mythical monsters influenced artists of the Greco-Roman period, which spanned the years 332 B.C. to A.D. 395.

The Japanese seahorse is called *sangotatsu* in Japan, which means "one who stands like a coral."

Left to right: sculpture in Phuket, Thailand; King Croesus's brooch in Turkey; iron ring for tying up horses in Italy

Rome. The fountain is 86 feet (26.2 m) tall and about 161 feet (49.1 m) wide. It took 30 years to complete. In 1926, Italian prime minister Benito Mussolini gave the American people a gift to celebrate the nation's 150th birthday. *The Fountain of the Seahorses*, located in Philadelphia, is a replica of a fountain in Rome. Four hippocamps, each weighing 5,000 pounds (2,268 kg), hold up a shallow bowl that weighs about 16,000 pounds (7,257 kg).

Another piece of hippocamp art is a huge plate, called the Great Dish. Part of the Mildenhall Treasure, a fourth-century Roman collection, the Great Dish depicts a celebration attended by gods, sea nymphs, the hero Hercules, and many mythical creatures, including hippocamps. The plate, which is made of solid silver,

is nearly 2 feet (0.6 m) across and weighs more than 18 pounds (8.2 kg). Around the seventh century, in what is now Turkey, people known as Lydians crafted exquisite gold jewelry. A brooch made in the shape of a winged hippocamp was designed for a king named Croesus. The brooch remained hidden until Croesus's tomb was discovered in 1966, when it was put into a Turkish museum. Worth millions of dollars, the brooch was stolen from the museum in 2005. In 2013, it was found in Germany and returned to Turkey.

Hippocamps made their way to Scotland with invading Romans, where a tribe of people known as the Picts adopted hippocamps into their mythology. From the sixth through the ninth centuries, the Picts

Left to right: sculpture in Puerto Vallarta, Mexico; carved seahorse with Turkish eye, symbol of Cyprus; close-up view of the Great Dish

POSEIDON'S HIPPOCAMPS

Now Zeus, when he had brought the Trojans and Hector to the ships, left the combatants there to have toil and woe unceasingly, but himself turned away his bright eyes, and looked afar, upon the land of the Thracian horsemen, and of the Mysians that fight in close combat, and of the lordly Hippemolgi that drink the milk of mares, and of the Abii, the most righteous of men. To Troy he no longer in any wise turned his bright eyes, for he deemed not in his heart that any of the immortals would draw nigh to aid either Trojans or Danaans. But the lord, the Shaker of Earth [Poseidon], kept no blind watch, for he sat marvelling at the war and the battle, high on the topmost peak of wooded Samothrace, for from thence all Ida was plain to see; and plain to see were the city of Priam, and the ships of the Achaeans. There he sat, being come forth from the sea, and he had pity on the Achaeans that they were overcome by the Trojans, and against Zeus was he mightily wroth. Forthwith then he went down from the rugged mount, striding forth with swift footsteps, and the

high mountains trembled and the woodland beneath the immortal feet of Poseidon as he went. Thrice he strode in his course, and with the fourth stride he reached his goal, even Aegae, where was his famous palace builded in the depths of the mere, golden and gleaming, imperishable for ever. Thither came he, and let harness beneath his car his two bronze hooved horses [hippocamps], swift of flight, with flowing manes of gold; and with gold he clad himself about his body, and grasped the well-wrought whip of gold, and stepped upon his car, and set out to drive over the waves. Then gambolled the sea-beasts beneath him on every side from out the deeps, for well they knew their lord, and in gladness the sea parted before him; right swiftly sped they on, and the axle of bronze was not wetted beneath; and unto the ships of the Achaeans did the prancing steeds bear their lord.

From Book XIII of The Illiad, *by Homer; trans. by A. T. Murray, 1924*

carved images of people and creatures—including hippocamps—into tall stone monuments, called steles. Dozens of steles still exist, though most have been moved from their original locations to museums throughout Great Britain. The image of the seahorse as a magical creature persisted through the centuries. In the 12th century, the Celts of northern Europe and the British Isles adopted the hippocamp as a symbol of their people's strength and perseverance. Believing that seahorses brought good luck, Celtic sailors carried hippocamp carvings as magical charms.

Across much of northern Europe, people believed that if a sailor died at sea, hippocamps would safely guide the sailor's soul to the underworld. In Great Britain, the hippocamp's front hooves were changed to webbed feet, and the dorsal fin became much longer. This image has been incorporated into numerous **coats of arms**. The hippocamp is still present on the crests of the city of Belfast, Northern Ireland; England's Isle of Wight and cities of Newcastle upon Tyne and Cambridge; Carmarthenshire in Wales; Australia's University of Newcastle; and countless other places. The hippocamp

The large area covered by the Thames Estuary is perhaps why seahorses were not found there until recently.

Short- and long-snouted seahorses live in the cool, muddy waters where England's River Thames meets the North Sea.

The manaia was tasked with looking after a person's spirit in life and then serving as the spirit's guide after death.

Unlike other seahorses, the paradoxical seahorse has no dorsal fin and instead has 8 to 10 pectoral fins along its back and tail.

is an enduring symbol of strength, safety, and the importance of human connections to the sea.

Many Pacific Island **cultures** include seahorses in their traditions and mythologies. The Mãori people of New Zealand call the seahorse *manaia*, which is also the name of a magical creature believed to ward off evil and protect people from danger. Seahorses have long been important images included in the Mãori traditions of *tã moko*, which is the carving of patterns in the skin, and tattooing— still important means of cultural identity for the Mãori people. Seahorses were dried and worn as necklaces for good luck, and charms carved out of bone or wood in the shape of the manaia were also worn. The manaia design is still an important Mãori symbol today.

Seahorses in drawings and paintings have captured people's imaginations for centuries. The 15th-century German printmaker Daniel Hofper was one of the first people to use etched metal plates in printmaking. One of his prints was a seahorse. Four hundred years later, American painter and illustrator Frederick Stuart Church created an etching of a mermaid riding a seahorse. British naturalist John Josselyn saw seahorses in the New World in

1672 and, two years later, wrote in his book *An Account of the Voyages to New England* that they reminded him of the dragon in the famous 11th-century British story of Saint George, who killed a dragon that terrorized a village.

Modern fictional seahorses are not quite as fanciful or fierce. Stormy the Giant Seahorse is a character in *The Little Mermaid* television series, which ran from 1992 to 1994 on the Disney Channel. Stormy was captured as a wild seahorse, and Ariel tried to tame him. But Stormy was too wild at heart, so King Triton and Ariel set him free. A more civilized seahorse made an appearance in the television show *SpongeBob SquarePants*. A green seahorse named Mystery was featured in a 2002 episode titled "My Pretty Seahorse." Mystery led SpongeBob through a series of mishaps and then mysteriously disappeared, never to be seen or heard from again. She did, however, reappear in the 2003 SpongeBob video game *Battle for Bikini Bottom*. Real-life seahorses are featured in a number of online videos presented by aquariums around the world, including Monterey Bay Aquarium in California, Mystic Aquarium in Connecticut, and the California Academy of Sciences in San Francisco, California.

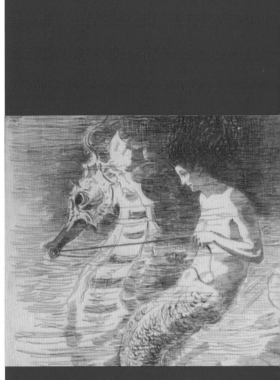

In 1880, American artist Frederick Stuart Church created "The Mermaid" for the magazine American Art Review.

The sea pony seahorse is native to the Red Sea, but in 2002, scientists found it had traveled to the Mediterranean through the Suez Canal.

No other fish species on the planet has a neck—the seahorse is unique in that respect.

SEAHORSES IN JEOPARDY

More than 200 different species of pipefish exist, typically sharing habitats with their seahorse cousins.

T he first seahorses **evolved** from their pipefish relatives. In 2010, scientists at the University of Antwerp in Belgium learned how pipefish and seahorses diverged from a common pipefish ancestor. It has to do with how these fish catch prey. Both fish need to be very close to a prey animal to suck it up in their tube-mouth. The researchers observed that the seahorse's curved neck allows it to reach farther to capture food than pipefish are able to reach. Pipefish swim toward their prey, while seahorses, with their anchoring tails, remain motionless as prey comes to them. Their bodies evolved into an S-shape, which allows seahorses to reach farther from a stationary position to nab prey.

The seahorse's development likely occurred in the coastal seagrass beds of the shallow Paratethys Sea, which once covered what is now Central Europe and parts of Central Asia. Fossils of two early seahorse species were discovered in 2005 in Slovenia by Jure Žalohar, who was a student at the University of Ljubljana at the time. The *Hippocampus sarmaticus* fossil was about two inches (5.1 cm) long, and two juvenile *Hippocampus slovenicus* fossils

Longsnout seahorses (not to be confused with long-snouted seahorses) inhabit coastal waters from North Carolina to central Brazil.

With spots like its namesake, the giraffe seahorse can be found in coastal waters of Tanzania, Mozambique, and South Africa.

each measured less than a quarter of an inch (0.6 cm) long. At 13 million years old, these fossils are the oldest seahorses ever found. Discovering the tiny fossils was pure luck for Žalohar, who was not even looking for them. He had been jogging and stopped at a stream to wash his hands. Kneeling down among broken plates of gray siltstone, Žalohar spotted the fossils.

A similar stroke of luck led to the discovery of the first pygmy seahorses ever recorded. In 1969, marine biologist George Bargibant was studying sea fans for the Nouméa Aquarium in New Caledonia. He would not have noticed the pair of half-inch-long (1.3 cm) seahorses if they had not let go of the sea fan and begun swimming. At first, Bargibant thought pieces of the sea fan had broken off, but upon closer inspection, he realized the bits of floating pink-speckled material were actually tiny fish. After a year of studying the creatures, they were given a name: Bargibant's pygmy seahorse. It would be 30 years before another species of pygmy seahorse was discovered. Once scientists understood what to look for and where to look, more pygmy seahorses were found. By 2009, seven pygmy species had been named.

Denise's pygmy seahorse, first described in 2003, has been spotted near Indonesia, Palau, Malaysia, the Solomon Islands, and Micronesia.

Trawling is one of the most destructive fishing practices today because it destroys seabed habitats.

Along with the discovery that new seahorse species exist has come the realization that they are in danger. Seahorses face a number of major threats—all caused by humans. As human activity accelerates global climate change, ocean temperatures rise. Even slight changes in the environment can have harmful effects on seahorses, increasing their chances of disease and **parasites**, and affecting their abilities to feed and reproduce. Seahorses are also targets of commercial trades. Few seahorse species reproduce in captivity, so most seahorses sold as pets are taken from the wild. As many as one million seahorses are captured for the aquarium trade each year, and only 1 in 1,000 survives in captivity more than 6 weeks.

Another one million seahorses are captured as souvenirs. Their bodies are dried out and made into keychains, jewelry, ornaments, and other trinkets to be sold to tourists around the world.

Commercial fishing takes a toll on seahorses as well. Trawling is a practice in which huge nets are weighed down and dragged across the seabed for miles. The goal is to capture shrimp, but for every 1 pound (0.5 kg) of shrimp collected, 10 pounds (4.5 kg) of other animals are pulled up from the floor as well. These creatures, called bycatch, have no commercial value to the fishermen. Often dead or dying from injuries, they are tossed overboard. Trawling is one of the biggest threats to seahorses. Every year, trawlers drag their nets across an area of seabed twice the size of the continental United States. Not only do trawlers catch and kill millions of seahorses and other marine creatures, but they also destroy the habitats of these animals.

Equally alarming to conservationists is the use of seahorses in traditional Asian medicines. More than 90 different products sold as medicine in China and other parts of Asia contain seahorses. Although no scientific evidence exists to prove their medicinal value, millions of seahorses

Project Seahorse invites visitors to their iSeahorse website to share photos of seahorses they have encountered.

In most species, male and female seahorses are the same color, but male slender seahorses are orange, while females are yellow.

Seahorses are particularly sensitive to changes in water quality and temperature—both factors affected by climate change.

are captured each year and made into powders and pills that are eaten to cure various dysfunctions and diseases. Researchers with the Seahorse Trust, a British conservation organization, found that seahorse populations have plummeted by 50 percent since 2010. They estimate that if humans continue to harvest seahorses at the current rate, these animals could completely die out by the year 2045.

Perhaps no one has done more to protect seahorses than marine biologists Dr. Amanda Vincent and Dr. Heather Koldewey. In 1996, these scientists founded Project Seahorse, an organization dedicated to the education of fishermen and people who harvest seahorses and the training of future conservationists. Project Seahorse also conducts research and works on conservation programs. Dr. Vincent was the first person to study seahorses underwater in the wild, and she is considered the world's foremost authority on these animals. Her research led the Convention on International Trade in Endangered Species (CITES) to adopt trade controls for all seahorse species in 2002. While Japan, Indonesia, South Korea, and Norway refused to sign the agreement, other nations made the trade of wild seahorses either limited or completely illegal.

Prior to the CITES agreement, as many as 150 million seahorses were taken from the sea annually. The current estimate is now around 20 million a year—mostly from illegal fishing and commercial bycatch. More protections are needed if seahorses are to avoid extinction. Despite intense research conducted by scientists from Project Seahorse, the John G. Shedd Aquarium in Chicago, and many other conservation organizations, little is known about the lives of seahorses in the wild. These remarkable creatures are truly unique in the animal kingdom and possess a host of amazing secrets—if only they can survive long enough to reveal them to us.

In 2014, scientists at Brazil's Universidade Estadual da Paraíba learned that seahorses growl when handled.

ANIMAL TALE: THE WATER HORSE OF WALES

In A.D. 43, Rome began its conquest of England. The invading Romans brought with them various cultural influences, including their legendary creatures. In what is today southern Wales, the mythical Roman hippocamp became a water horse called Ceffyl Dwr (*KETCH-ih DOOR*). The 2010 discovery of short-snouted seahorses in the coastal waters of Wales renders this nearly 2,000-year-old Welsh legend almost believable today.

In the old days, people often walked long distances through dark and fearsome landscapes. One such place that unlucky travelers sometimes found themselves was the Afon Ysbrydion (*a-VON esp-YED-ee-on*), or the Haunted River. This was the dwelling place of Ceffyl Dwr, a shapeshifting spirit that did not like strangers in his territory. Sometimes he stood on the riverbank as a tall, white horse with a flowing mane and four strong legs. Other times he swam in the river, his back legs transformed into the body of a fish with a long, curled tail. And sometimes he was a thin, cool mist that drifted from the river to spend nights on the seashore nearby.

A man had been walking for many days when he unknowingly came upon the Haunted River. He spied a row of huge, flat stones that made a sort of bridge by which he could cross the fast-moving water. But he was very tired and afraid he would not make it across the river safely until after he rested, so he settled under a tree and went to sleep.

When he awoke, the man saw the sun was nearly on the horizon. He thought he should try to hurry across the river before dark. As he stood up and slung his pack over his shoulder, he heard a noise nearby. There on the riverbank stood a magnificent white horse. It was the finest horse the man had ever seen. *If only I could catch that horse*, he thought, *I could ride it across the river and for the rest of my journey as well*.

The man stepped toward the horse. The big animal seemed unafraid, which encouraged the man to draw closer. He reached out his hand to the horse, but it did not flee. *This is wonderful*, thought the man. And in one swift motion, he leapt upon the horse's back and clutched the animal's long mane in both hands.

Gently, he guided the horse toward the river's edge, elated that he was now the owner of this fine steed. But the moment the horse's hooves left the sandy riverbank, the horse raced headlong into the swirling water. Its back legs melted and transformed into the glistening body of a fish, and its tail curled into a spiral.

Astonished, the man shouted for the horse to stop, but before he could finish his cry, he was pulled beneath the surface of the dark water, where he disappeared, never to be seen again. Rising from the river, riderless and eyes blazing, the white horse was transformed into a mist that drifted on the wind toward the sea.

Considering this story today, perhaps when the mist settled on the seashore, the Ceffyl Dwr transformed once again. Perhaps he remains in the seagrass meadows in the shallow waters off the coast of Wales. A master of shapeshifting, perhaps he can be seen to this day as the short-snouted seahorse.

GLOSSARY

buoyancy – the ability to float in water

camouflage – the ability to hide, due to coloring or markings that blend in with a given environment

climate change – any long-term change of pattern in the planet's or a region's atmosphere, environments, and long-term weather conditions

coats of arms – the official symbols of a family, state, nation, or other group

contaminants – non-natural substances that have a negative effect upon the environment or animals

cultures – particular groups in a society that share behaviors and characteristics that are accepted as normal by that group

ecosystem – a community of organisms that live together in an environment

estuaries – the mouths of large rivers, where the tides (from oceans or seas) meet the streams

evolved – gradually developed into a new form

glands – organs in a human or animal body that produce chemical substances used by other parts of the body

hormones – chemical substances produced in the body that control and regulate the activity of certain cells and organs

membranes – thin, clear layers of tissue that cover internal organs or developing organisms

mosaics – pictures or designs made by arranging small pieces of colored material such as glass, stone, or tile

mythology – a collection of myths, or popular, traditional beliefs or stories that explain how something came to be or that are associated with a person or object

nutrients – substances that give an animal energy and help it grow

parasites – animals or plants that live on or inside another living thing (called a host) while giving nothing back to the host; some parasites cause disease or even death

pigments – materials or substances present in the tissues of animals or plants that give them their natural coloring

prehensile – capable of grasping

zooplankton – tiny sea creatures (some microscopic) and the eggs and larvae of larger animals

SELECTED BIBLIOGRAPHY

ARKive. "Spiny Seahorse (*Hippocampus histrix*)." http://www.arkive.org/spiny-seahorse/hippocampus-histrix.

Gilpin, Daniel, Amy-Jane Beer, and Derek Hall. *The Illustrated Encyclopedia of Fish & Shellfish of the World*. London: Lorenz Books, 2010.

Indiviglio, Frank. *Seahorses: Everything About History, Care, Nutrition, Handling, and Behavior*. Hauppauge, N.Y.: Barron's, 2002.

Project Seahorse. "Research Programs." http://www.projectseahorse.org/research-programs.

Scales, Helen. *Poseidon's Steed: The Story of Seahorses, from Myth to Reality*. New York: Gotham Books, 2009.

U.S. Fish & Wildlife Service: International Affairs. "Seahorses." http://www.fws.gov/international/animals/sea-horses.html.

Note: Every effort has been made to ensure that any websites listed above were active at the time of publication. However, because of the nature of the Internet, it is impossible to guarantee that these sites will remain active indefinitely or that their contents will not be altered.

Perhaps new and different seahorse species are still hidden in the ocean depths, waiting to be discovered.

INDEX